T0195957

THE WORLD IN YOUR HANDS

ADVANCED GUIDE TO PALMISTRY COUNSELLING

Professional Edition

John Harrison

authorHOUSE®

AuthorHouse™ UK
1663 Liberty Drive
Bloomington, IN 47403 USA
www.authorhouse.co.uk
Phone: 0800 047 8203 (Domestic TFN)
    +44 1908 723714 (International)

Published by AuthorHouse 07/18/2019

ISBN: 978-1-7283-8938-7 (sc)
ISBN: 978-1-7283-8939-4 (e)

CONTENTS

FIGURES

PREFACE

Palmistry counselling is a wonderful and fascinating career option. As everyone, in all parts of the world has hands, being human, the potential rewards, for the disciplined, caring, intuitive professional are great. Both personally, and in my career, I have travelled the world, met amazing and truly awe inspiring people from many diverse cultures and had the privilege, but also responsibility, to read their hands.

Both attention and intention are important criterion for the successful palmistry counsellor. Under ideal circumstances, a positive belief system is helpful. I have had the enormous pleasure of meeting people from different races, different faiths, and different lifestyles. For me, both personally and professionally, it is essential that I endorse the positive beliefs of my clients. Being both a humanitarian and life-long spiritual aspirant this is an integral part of my lifestyle.

In practice, you could use this book to learn palmistry counselling and with practice, follow me and become well-established, respected and earn a good living in this field. Yes, it is significant that this is a career option, but like any job, it requires the acquisition of skills, preferably many years of education and putting such knowledge into practice.

Presently, you have to be a person with intuitive gifts. Personally, I have experience of clairvoyance, clairsentience, psychokinesis, telepathy and healing. Often, most regrettably, I know from experience that such abilities are not always welcomed in society. My own childhood, although generally happy, was marred by grief and loneliness; especially on those occasions when I tried to explain to my parents that my grandparents were not dead but existing in a parallel dimension, filled with light. Paradoxically, from my teenage years, I took a great interest in religions, especially those from the East.

Therefore, both for my students and in collaboration with supportive colleagues, I feel qualified to proffer the following advice and guidance concerning the correct ethical standards to adhere to in dealings with the general public.

Firstly, you will meet atheists, agnostics and those of faith.

Treat each person with respect and honour their choices related to religion, as well as politics. It is wise to have a belief that enhances your lifestyle, so fully consider other people's well-being and seek to nurture their potential.

In the profession of palmistry counselling, it is essential to have a good working knowledge of chirology, also called hand analysis. Knowledge is at the core of our profession, so we need to know the "nuts and bolts". Both Dr Benham and Dr Charlotte Wolfe as well as Noel Jacquin were the modern pioneers of this discipline, which was then allied to medicine and psychology.

Therefore, if you are a "psychic", it is essential to get a good grounding in chirology in order to become a well rounded professional. Whilst, I know from experience that intuition and perception play an important role in any palmistry consultation, the honest truth is that psychic impressions are not always either forthcoming or reliable. If this should happen to you, when reading hands, and you have a knowledge of chirology, then your client will not be disappointed. Indeed, often when I have provided a client, perhaps with an extraordinarily accurate reading, they have declared that my psychic skills were amazing. However, often, in my own estimation of my skills, I inform clients, of the fact, that I have been reading their hands like they would read a book! I believe that the hands are, in part, an archive or library of all that has occurred in the past. In addition, the future trends are often rooted in both past and present actions, such that few people change radically. However, where such changes do occur, evidence of this can be perceived often in advance of the actual events.

For the therapist, or healer, palmistry counselling would complement their skills. Having read the hands of doctors, nurses, osteopaths, psychotherapists and healers, I know that their natural caring skills nearly always require intuitive skills. Although, they themselves would perhaps not agree that they are "psychic" or have spiritual gifts, my observation is that the majority of medical practitioners and those in the holistic medicine fields do possess such abilities, albeit often in a latent form. So, does it therefore follow that "psychics" may be caring? Well, of course, that is often true. However, if asked whether chirologists are "psychic", or have caring skills, the answer is not so clear. Indeed, chirologists, often being grounded in science, can be very critical and judgemental of "psychics". They believe in science, rather than philosophy or alchemy [Magic]?

Why did I found and create the profession of palmistry counselling? The reason for my life's work, and my 35 year career, is because I recognised there was a need for it. Regrettably, we learn, principally, because of a shared history in that we are all descended from hominids. Some of the earliest religions were matriarchal, based upon the worship of goddesses. These earlier pagan faiths also introduced us to mythology and philosophy. We know that Romany Gypsies travelled from India and that their knowledge was ancient, based upon the Shastras in the Vedas.

With the decline of paganism and its worship of ancestors, spirits and nature, the later faiths were more paternalistic. Over time, the divine feminine became subjugated to the divine masculine, and alchemy, hermeticism and magic were superseded by science, which is now promulgated as containing the only truths?

With the coming of the industrial revolution, nature was finally conquered and we all became the unwilling servants of the so called "captains of industry". The corporations and industries that have been created are primarily interested in power and money. We are ruled by science and technology. From cradle to grave, our lives are often governed by an unelected elite, who pay little heed to the itinerant populations, and most specifically the human rights of what has been labelled the "common people", from whom we are all descended! Fortunately, with globalisation and the rise of social media, our freedoms and human rights can be addressed which should lead to injustices being reversed.

INTRODUCTION TO PALMISTRY COUNSELLING AS A CAREER

Providing that you have the basic skills in counselling; are observant, perceptive, intuitive and have common sense then a career in palmistry counselling could be your profession. If you have studied chirology from books, learnt via online training or from a competent teacher, these skills are adequate. Alternatively, you may at present be a therapist, which in my view, would increase the likelihood of you being intuitive. So, all you have to do is get a good grounding in hand analysis. For the psychic, my experience informs me that you are probably a caring person because psychics seek to serve their clients and often possess counselling skills. Therefore, my advice would be to study the books on palmistry and chirology, and then use that knowledge in your consultations.

I especially encourage women and those from ethnic origins to seriously consider the profession of palmistry counselling. Indian people who have studied the Vedas or anyone who has studied esoteric philosophy have a wonderful archive of knowledge to call upon. When we consider the origins of palmistry, there were illustrious pioneers such as Paracelsus, Cornelius Agrippa and Robert Fludd, and even geniuses such as Sir Isaac Newton, who portrayed the angelic realms!

In modern times, Carl Jung, understood the need for archetypes.

Therefore, in order to gain a deeper knowledge and wisdom, I actively encourage my many students to explore hermetic philosophy, alchemy, metaphysical heurism and ontology. Here there is a veritable treasure of beautiful imagery, wonderful philosophy, from which my own preference stretches back to Hermes Trismegistus, wherein is enshrined "the wisdom of the ages"!

Whilst we should acknowledge and respect the achievements of scientists, since the industrial revolution, in palmistry counselling we need to ground our intellectual perception in ancient wisdom. Long before astronomy and the space age of exploration, our ancestors were gazing at the stars and galaxies with a sense of awe and humility that is perhaps lost in this modern technological age.

It is for this reason that I recommend modern palmistry counsellors to gain insights into astrology and numerology. In addition, for the committed spiritual aspirant, a good understanding of sacred geometry and metaphysics is essential.

PRACTICAL AIDS TO OUR PROFESSION

Firstly, you may need premises from which to work. This could be your home or you chose to rent a suitable room. Professionally, you may work at psychic fairs or mind body soul exhibitions. Generally, for outside events a Gazebo or Marquee may be needed. Of course, you may be invited to corporate events or charity shows.

Most psychics and chirologists know that party bookings are a potentially lucrative and enjoyable way to earn a living serving the public. For corporate events, such as Christmas Parties or conferences, in your marketing, as well as in the presentation of your services, you will need a plan in advance and be appropriately dressed. Here, I provide you with an insight into the corporate mindset.

Whilst it is true, that regrettably many people in public life have strong opinions about the merits of psychics and therefore by association palmistry counsellors, provided that you are psychologically well prepared plus able to remain calm and respectful then such prejudices as you may encounter can be diffused. Fortunately, gone are the days when any person's human rights could be abused without consequences.

Nowadays, the professional entrepreneur has professional indemnity insurance and may belong to an association, such as the Spiritual Workers Association, which may protect their interests legally. However, never forget to prominently display your Disclaimer which details the provisions of your services. Remember professional courtesy and integrity. Previously, when invited to attend corporate events, I knew in advance that my recruitment was essentially for entertainment purposes. Therefore, it is important to present the correct demeanor, preferably with a self-deprecating sense of humour and charm.

In the early days, often the partner of a CEO, or Managing Director would come for a private consultation and then recommend my services to her husband. Equally, on one occasion at a Christmas Party, I read the hands exclusively of female executives managing a division of Virgin Media. The hosts at this event were wonderful and my clients seemed happy with my services.

However, a word of caution is needed in this regard. At any event, where men and women congregate, often large amounts of alcohol can be consumed in a party setting. I recommend however, that you, as a palmistry counsellor avoid consumption on such occasions. Otherwise, there is the ever present danger that the boundaries between employer and palmistry counsellor may become blurred leading potentially to compromising situations.

Equally, remember that all consultations are private and confidential.

BUSINESS REQUIREMENTS

In order to practice this therapy professionally, you will require business credentials, including signage, business stationery, advertising materials such as leaflets and business cards. If feasible hire a good chartered accountant and/ or bookkeeper to handle your financial affairs. It is also wise to employ a good firm of lawyers to protect your interests. Ensure that you have valid professional indemnity insurance. If you attend exhibitions, you may need a portable table, pop-up display banner and some device to record consultations. As even CD recorders are now outdated, often I would suggest to clients that they record the palmistry consultation on their mobile phone. Equally, you should have the means to take payments either via a laptop or credit card machine.

An important factor in your professional life is to have a good website, excellent SEO and either yourself or professionals should actively market your services on the internet and social media channels. Both radio and TV appearances plus regular articles in leading magazines will help raise your profile so that the general public are aware of their value. In terms of professional conduct, although it is often an advantage to create a distinct image via clothing, you may need to adapt this aspect appropriately, depending on the venue.

You will need to get organised and must be prepared to pay exhibition organisers on time in order to book your stand. Try to dovetail your own promotion of your services with their marketing campaigns; indeed actively help promote them. You will probably need a reliable car in order to travel to work venues; plus book accomodation for weekend work assignments well in advance. List these in your diary, on a laptop or mobile phone.

To be charming and have a good sense of humour are invaluable personality traits. My experience informs me that possessing a testimonials book plus interesting leaflets and great signage with visible links to your website and Facebook account are important aspects for your success. Although you may have been a psychic, therapist or chirologist, remember that you have now chosen to become a palmistry counsellor, and this has many advantages over any other stand holders.

Remember, that although your desire is to serve and be caring, compassionate, diplomatic and actively seek for your clients to become self-empowered and self-actuated, thereby living happy, prosperous and fulfilling lives, you may have to learn to market and sell your services effectively.

In any professional setting in which you have agreed to work and abided by the regulations of management, or hosts, it is both acceptable and desirable to sell your services enthusiastically.

For myself, although in one sense exhibitions could be viewed as a place containing competitors as each person needs to earn a living, my own approach was to co-operate with other professionals. Indeed, I actively pursued free networking opportunities, and shared openly information about other exhibitions. Remember, that not only the general public but also other stand holders may be interested in your services. Therefore, always hand out leaflets to them and possibly offer them a discount if they come and see you on your stand?

Whilst one option would be to hand out leaflets to every member of the public passing by your stand, a better policy could be to ask them to read your testimonials, remaining silent, then answering their questions. Equally, they may choose to read a magazine article written about your services in a prominent magazine. I also thoroughly recommend and endorse the use of free talks or paid for workshops where you could tell others about yourself and your therapy in a relaxed setting. Although the way you market yourself is very much an individual choice, be aware that at exhibitions you only have a limited time to sell your skills, so be focused and disciplined.

Most people who have worked professionally in any type of sales job will tell you that often you are the service or product; in other words, if someone likes and trusts you then they will buy from you. So, even if you are tired, having a bad day, or feeling ill, always smile, for as the old song goes, "when you are smiling, the whole world smiles with you".

Finally, be confident and self-assured.

Most people will on occasion feel insecure or vulnerable and there is not a person born who does not, at some stage, experience setbacks and suffering; but remember that every person can have courage in adversity. Personally and professionally, I always loved my work.

Having travelled the world, and read the hands of people from diverse cultures, religions, or those choosing alternative lifestyles, I have learnt to have a humanitarian love for most of my clients that underpins my career. Whilst to err, make mistakes or sin is human. My choice is to be kind, caring, compassionate and understanding, as far as is humanly possible.

Belief is the single most important factor in your career and your life. Believe in yourself as a person of worth. Believe in other people where their philosophy is imbued with love, compassion and forgiveness. Believe in God, if possible, and have humility. It is not always necessary to be religious; I have met many truly wonderful agnostics and atheists and been supportive of their opinions but endeavour to meditate, or pray, as that is a great solace in times of need. Whilst, it is not necessary to believe to become a good palmistry counsellor, it certainly helps to remain open-minded and listen attentively to the needs of others. In this way, you can better serve them.

INTRODUCTION

Chirology is the analytical study hands. Palmistry is but one aspect of a greater system, namely alchemy. Philosophically this system sought to explain man's spiritual transmutation from matter to spiritual-enlightenment.

The human hand has more sensory endings than any other part of the body. Certain experts maintain that it conveys our logical thinking and emotional perception from the brain to the physical hand.

A brief historical scenario: Chirology commenced its development in India where it was and is studied in connection with vedic astrology. A leading exponent in the West was Cheiro, a great seer.

The method of palmistry counselling I utilise is compiled from serious study of authorities, and from research and observation in human society.

A THE PHYSIOLOGY

This has its root in chirology, and in the Karmic Law of Cause and Effect. A person is affected by many external aspects, namely environment, work, geographical location, family, position etc. and also physical factors, e.g.; genetics, the position of bones, blood vessels, metabolism etc. Skin formation also determines a person's state of health – dermatoglyphics.

B THE PSYCHOLOGY

A person's thoughts, feelings and emotions are etched into the palm, in a similar way to that in which an artist paints a picture, having colour, tone, depth and meaning. From these lines we can interpret a person's balances and imbalances, strengths and weaknesses. Thus chirology examines human potential. From this we can give direction to a person and indicate setbacks.

C CHIROGNOMY and CHIROMANCY

These are the "nuts and bolts" of our craft. The former studies the formation of the hand – its human mould. Whether the hand is thin or flabby, large or small, weathered or malformed will all show up in chirognomy.

Chiromancy studies the palmar regions. It examines the handprint and lines, noting length, depth, vacillation etc., also skin temperature and complexion.

Lastly, the hand may be viewed as an energy field or "Window of the Soul". In this aspect it receives and transmits vibrations. Some people make you "feel good"; others strike you as "touchy". Herein intuition plays a vital role. Clairvoyants claim that they can read the aura of a person.

To conclude, I do not expect you to believe in palmistry counselling ; it is not a form of magic. Be curious, sceptical, critical; most of all desire to know the truth, in order to discover yourself. Knowledge plus application equal success. Dare to know?

THE GEOGRAPHY OF THE PALM

When reading a map, a navigator looks for certain landmarks to indicate his position in relation to his surroundings. He may also use a technical instrument, namely a compass or possibly a sextant. This analogy is true of scientific palmistry. A chirologist tries to chart a course for a person's life, indicating opportunities as well as possible turbulent times. A person should have their hand read on several occasions during life because we are granted free will, and as we change our course, so may our lives alter.

Let us firstly analyse the shape of the hand. The outer hand represents to the world that which we wish to convey. Notice any hair. On the hand of a man indicates virility: the converse makes a man more sensitive and perhaps artistic. Note bone structure and if possible hold the hand from below and feel its weight. Where do you suppose the term "heavy handed" came from? Notice any knotty joints for these interfere with the flow of energy from the brain. They indicate reason and discrimination but may also indicate an argumentative nature.

Next turn to the fingertips. Especially note if the tips are over-rounded and bulbous – this may indicate lung problems, heart weakness, or simply mineral deficiency. Observe if the fingers cling to one another or fold over one another – this shows caution, secretiveness and a desire to protect. Often this indicates inhibitions, self-doubt and lack of confidence. A wide spacing between the fingers argues well for a balanced person. Too wide spread illustrates great versatility but may place a strain upon a person because they may seek to overstretch their capacity, resulting in potential, nervous, disposition caused by trying to do too much. Without a well-proportioned thumb this could be an indication of mental illness.

Finally, consider the finger nails. When bitten they show nervousness and possibly lack of caution in matters relating to their to diet; flecked nails indicate bad circulation. In connection with this note the "moons", if lacking this person's health may be finely balanced. Note grooved nails. These could be an early sign of bronchitis or pleurisy – does the person smoke? Over long nails may indicate a covetous nature, curiosity is pronounced and a greedy approach to life may be found.

Let us now examine the inward hand. The palm which complements the outer one. Strangely, if the other hand appears large and the palm is small this shows deception. Especially note the thumb – this is truly the compass of the palm - the steering wheel of destiny. It should be at an angle of 45 degrees to the palm; herein it shows a balanced nature. A long close-held thumb shows caution and a person of discrimination; this person appreciates aesthetic objects; ideas of beauty appeal to the subject plus abstract thought.

A low set, wide-angled thumb shows physical aptitude and is atavistic; dancers, acrobats and athletes often have this setting. People with clubbed (short, thick upper phalanges of the thumb)may have suppressed frustration or anger. If present on hands, instinctive unresolved passions are indicated, and with a short head line, the potential for violence. When found on both the left and right hands, this can be an indication of potential criminal tendencies, especially as related to sexual abuse. However if only found on one hand, it could simply be an expression of restrained aggression. Notice the shape of the palm. Longer and thinner palms indicate mental agility or emotional responsiveness. Rounded palms show imagination and intuition.

SKIN RIDGE PATTERNS

Firstly, feel the skin; soft skin shows sensitivity, rougher skin indicates physicality. Notice if the palm is flat or undulating. The latter shows greater depth of emotion and qualities of life.

MOUNTS

Notice the mounts. When high and wide these illustrate possible talents; this is also true of fingerprint patterns.

Now turn to the lines. When deep and straight, they show objectivity – a person herein has clearly defined goals. However, this may lead to narrow-mindedness. Smooth, curving lines, especially the line of the heart, indicate a compassionate and sympathetic nature. Pleasure will be gained subjectively from the contents of life. Many lines on the hand indicate activity, few lines indicates a greater control over life and a simpler outlook.

This in brief indicates the geography of the palm, which in future sections will be expanded upon.

ARCHETYPES OF CHIROLOGY

Chirology finds its origins in the India Sanskrit Vedas, written 2000 years before Christ. Proponents of the Western tradition of chirology are guided by the works of Cornelius Agrippa (1483 – 1533), Paracelsus (1493 – 1541) and Robert Fludd (1574 – 1637). We also know that Socrates, Aristotle and Alexander the Great studied or wrote works on chiromancy. The philosophy that evolved from these teachings was Hermetic, deriving from the legendary figure Hermes Trismegistus, whose esoteric writings, lost in the mists of time, have been associated with the pharoahs of Egypt, then latterly, both greek and roman philosophy. To learn more on this subject, I recommend the following book , "The Hermetica -The Lost Wisdom of the Pharoahs"by Timothy Freake & Peter Candy.

Any serious student of mythology and religion will be aware of the sacred symbology linking the ancient worship of the Gods (Egyptian, Greek, Roman, Judaic and Christian) with the modern philosophies of recent centuries. At the heart of these beliefs lies the relation between God and Man between Spirit and Matter. Our world was created by the Word of God, which is represented in every religion since time immemorial.

In the Hermetic Philosophy of Cornelius Aggrippa the universe is composed of three worlds, these being:

A **THE MENS WORLD** – The Divine Mind comprising the Angels and Archangels, which is known as the Intellectual World;

B **THE CELESTIAL WORLD** – associated with planetary ruler ships i.e; Jupiter, Venus, Mars, etc.;

C **THE ELEMENTAL WORLD** – concerned with material creation, and governed by the Elements EARTH -AIR- FIRE- WATER.

ASTRO-PALMISTRY

SYMBOLIC KEYS TO PALMISTRY

Essentially, chirology is governed by The Elemental World in its pragmatic symbolism, and the Celestial World in its inspiration. In practice there is a division between the Indian palmists who utilise the Vedic system, associated with eastern astrology and the western chirologists, e.g.; European, American, Canadian, who prefer the Celestial system of planetary symbolism, which can be used in conjunction with western astrology.

BELOW is a Table of references, relating to the qualities of Planetary Rulership.

THE SUN – **The Masculine Day Force**
- Light, power, authority, brilliance, creativity, dignity, charisma, fortune, fame, father
- Practical aspects: Masculine – public offices

MERCURY – **The Winged Messenger**
- Ideology, wisdom, intellect, knowledge, communication, invention, learning
- Practical aspects: Masculine – medicine, education, languages, health, procreation

VENUS – **Cupid – The Archer of Love**
- Love, passion, pleasure, partnerships, music, arts, sexuality, spiritual joy
- Practical aspects: Feminine –loving relationships, artistic and musical abilities "Joie de <u>Vivre</u>"

MARS – **The God of War**
- Force, strength, virility, aggression, bravery, dynamism, assertiveness
- Practical aspects: Masculine – courage in adversity, strength, anger, domination

THE MOON – **The Feminine Night Force**
- Feminine intuition, imagination, psychic abilities, illusions, drug addictions, madness
- Practical aspects: "Mysticism, spirituality, intuition, emotions, visions, delusions, passive strength, genius, subconscious mind

THE EARTH – **The Material World**
- Home, family, cultures, nations, conservation, nature, mother, life, hope, enlightenment, karma

- Practical aspects: World trade, peace, war, transformation, communications, life, death, journey of souls

JUPITER – **Bringer of Joy**
- Faith, philosophy, dignity, reverence, justice, expansion, compassion, aspiration, confidence, assertion
- Practical aspects: Government, ideology, egotism, dominion, ruler ship, truth

SATURN – **Father Time**
- Science, law, discipline, authority, respect, constraint, materialism, history
- Practical aspects: Success through perseverance, severity, traditions, customs, property, crafts, investment, inheritance

URANUS – **Lord of Change**
- Invention, perception, discovery, cataclysm, revolution, reincarnation, upheaval
- Practical aspects: Moving house, changing jobs, unexpected events, inspiration, drastic actions, sudden good fortune/tragedy

NEPTUNE – **The Mystic Sorcerer**
- Dreams, spirituality, serenity, illusions, fantasies, visions, revelations, magic, occultism
- Practical aspects: Premonitions, astral travel, psychic intuition delusions, religious fanaticism, subliminal education.

PLUTO – **The Underworld**
- Transformation, regeneration, re-birth, procreation, sexuality, secret knowledge
- Practical aspects: Criticism, research, insight, karma, enlightenment, nuclear forces, genetic engineering, sex education

ASTROLOGY SYMBOLS

Mercury, Sun, Moon and the Three Worlds

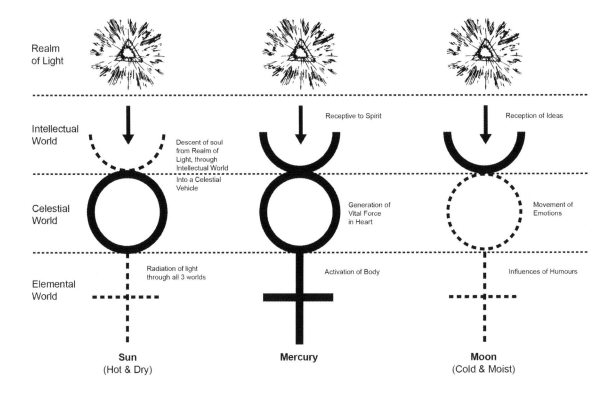

Realm of Light

Intellectual World

Receptive to Spirit

Reception of Ideas

Descent of soul from Realm of Light, through Intellectual World Into a Celestial Vehicle

Celestial World

Generation of Vital Force in Heart

Movement of Emotions

Radiation of light through all 3 worlds

Elemental World

Activation of Body

Influences of Humours

Sun
(Hot & Dry)

Mercury

Moon
(Cold & Moist)

Venus, Mars and the Three Worlds

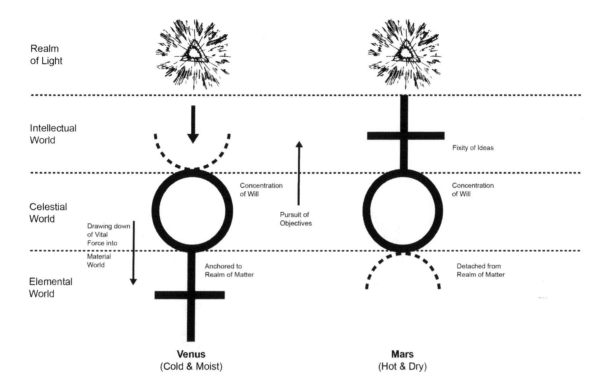

Saturn, Jupiter and the Three Worlds

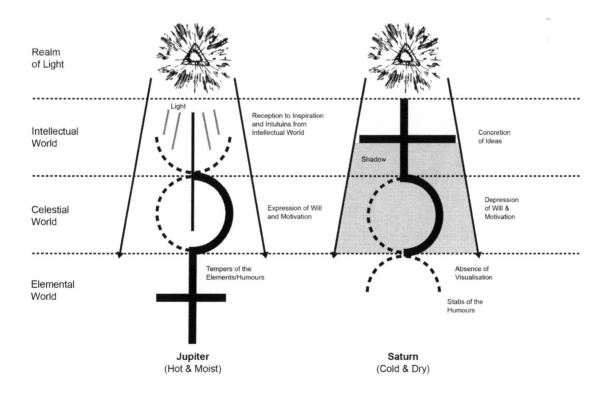

FIGURE ONE: ASTRO-PALMISTRY - Qualities of Phalanges

Compatability in relationships (personal and professional) depends upon Hand Chart Synastry to determine harmony by utilising a **Comparison Chart of Potentialities.**

Like Astrology, Palmistry can interpret.

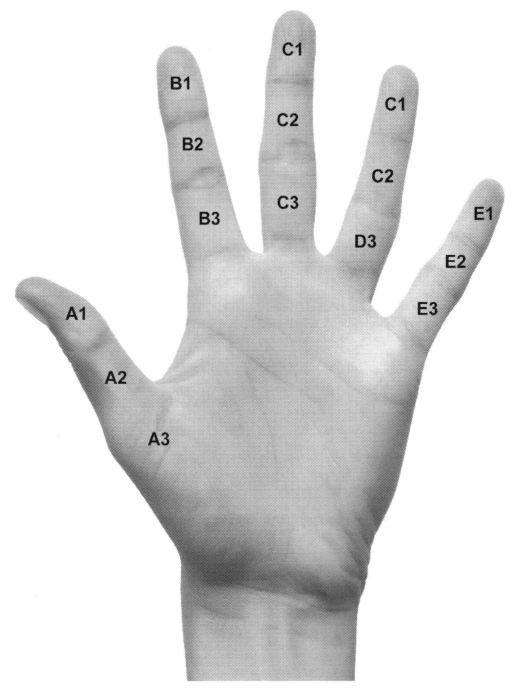

QUALITIES OF PHALANGES

THUMB	A1	Will-power, strength, energy
Mars	A2	Logic or sympathy
	A3	Passions (mount of Venus)

INDEX FINGER	B1	Faith, vision, idealism
Jupiter	B2	Management, confidence, accounting
	B3	Food, drink, money, power, sex

SECOND FINGER	C1	Law, science, philosophy, convention
Saturn	C2	Administration, timing, service, professional skills
	C3	Property, crafts, possessions, investment

THIRD FINGER	D1	Design, speech, education, creativity
Apollo	D2	Fashion, sports, entertainment, arts
	D3	Adventure, singing, dancing, pleasure-seeking

FOURTH FINGER	E1	Physics, magic, charisma, intuition
Mercury	E2	Literature, languages, finance, computing
	E3	Health, publishing, fertility, sex appeal

TABLE OF COMPATIBILITY

Winston Edwards	Client	Gloria Johnston
Speculate/Energetic	**Hand Type**	Intellectual/Philosophical
Loops	**Dominant Finger Prints**	Loops
Loops of Humour	**Palmar Prints**	Loops of Serious Intent
Mental Responsive	**Skin Type**	Energetic Responsive
Mars (Base) Apollo (Top) Jupiter (Top)	**Phalangeal Divisions (Largest)**	Saturn (Base) Jupiter (Base) Apollo (Middle)
Saturn (Top) Jupiter (Middle) Mercury (Middle)	**Phalangeal Divisions (Smallest)**	Jupiter (Top) Mar (Middle) Mercury (Top)
Mental Quality	**Major Lines**	Energetic Quality
Emotional Quality	**Minor Lines**	Emotional Quality

PSYCHOLOGY – THE PHALANGES INTERPRETED

(Refer to Figure One)

Through our finger phalanges we can gauge a person's psychological outlook.

For instance, a low-set finger of Mercury shows a tendency towards feelings of inferiority, or low self esteem. If the nail phalange curves inwards it indicates caution in speech, and possible deception, i.e.; a liar, or confidence trickster. Horizontal lines on the middle phalange of Mercury indicate a person who needs to be cautious with money.

When the middle phalange of Apollo is short or has horizontal lines it shows a tendency towards compulsive gambling.

The finger of Apollo shows our creative ideas. When the base phalange is tapered or short it is unfortunate; the person may be talented but they are physically incapable of becoming successful, as in when a person may love music but is unable to play. When the middle phalange of Apollo is long and wide it shows a love of order, excellent on a barrister's hand or that of any secretary.

When the nail phalange is short it shows someone incapable of appreciating beautiful works of art or pieces of music; it lends a mundane expression to the finger.

The finger of Saturn represents stability. It should be straight and inflexible. When the base phalange is wide and long it indicates abilities in engineering, electronics or practical science. A short middle phalange will be found on an untidy, impatient person or one inclined to gossip. A well- formed upper phalange gives person integrity; such a person will believe in a principle or cause and carry it out – however they may be inclined to be too serious.

Jupiter expresses our desire to expand our horizons. A large well- formed base phalange indicates an interest in food or a person who is a good cook. Alternatively it shows a person who likes to wield power. A good middle phalange, long and thin, shows a mathematical ability, possibly an accountant. A short upper phalange of Jupiter shows a fanatical nature, a zealous or reckless person.

These are some psychological insights into what a person's character may be interpreted as.

PROFESSIONAL INDICATIONS- THE FOLLOWING IS A TABLE OF CAREER OPTIONS

FINGER OF JUPITER

Base Phalange   Feminine/Complimentary

Farmers, shopkeepers, innkeepers, hoteliers, wine merchants and barristers, together with experts on nutrition, all have good phalanges.

Middle Phalange   Feminine/Opposition

Administrators, politicians, personal assistants, directors and professional soldiers/assassins all have good phalanges.

Nail Phalange   Feminine/Opposition

Artist, priests, pharmacologists, conservationists and those who pursue causes have good phalanges.

FINGER OF SATURN

Base Phalange   Feminine/Complimentary

Builders, engineers, biologist, prospectors, mathematicians, boxers and gardeners all have good phalanges.

Middle Phalange   Feminine/Opposition

Librarians, geologists, chemist, archaeologists, computer operators and electronics engineers have full phalanges.

Nail Phalange   Feminine/Opposition

Judges, philosophers, sociologists, psychiatrists, fine artists, interior, decorators and inventors have full phalanges.

FINGER OF APOLLO

Base Phalange   Masculine/Opposition

Acrobats, sportsmen, dancers, gamblers, landscape gardeners and bookmakers all have good lower phalanges.

Middle Phalange   Masculine/Complimentary

Ballet dancers, opera singers, tailors, artists, naval officers, musicians, designers and surgeons have good phalanges.

Nail Phalange Masculine/Complimentary

Charismatic leaders, comedians, composers, actors, poets, writers, sculptors and designers have fine phalanges.

FINGER OF MERCURY

Base Phalange Masculine/Opposition

Newscasters, journalists, doctors, nurses and pilots have strong base phalanges.

Middle Phalange Masculine/Complimentary

Singers, ventriloquists, linguists, accountants, bank managers, editors and veterinary surgeons have good phalanges.

Nail Phalange Masculine/Complimentary

Interpreters, literary critics, broadcasters, physiotherapists and experts in telecommunications and space flight have fine phalanges.

THE THUMB

Mount of Venus Matter/Spirit

Good mounts of Venus are found in the hands of athletes, composers and those who appreciate the spoken word.

Middle Thumb Phalange Executive Function

Organisers, co-ordinators, diplomats and the peacemakers all have good waisted thumbs.

Nail Thumb Phalange Administrative Function

Those in authority, particularly politicians, military leaders, lawyers and religious leaders have excellent phalanges.

FINGER AND THUMB ANALYSIS

BASE PHALANGES – **PRACTICAL WORLD**

Vertical lines show strengths. Many vertical lines, called hyper-striations indicate stress. On base phalanges these refer to the physical or materialistic.

Horizontal lines (bars) show inhibition, either internally, e.g.; how you act or externally, how others affect you.

MIDDLE PHALANGES – **ENERGETIC WORLD**

Vertical lines show abilities in the execution of organisational strategies.

Horizontal lines show mental inhibitions and doubts – lack of vision.

Externally: Your aptitudes as a responsible person – of work, managerial roles; at home, parental guidance and problem solving.

Internally: Your psychological strengths or weaknesses, at expressing yourself as an adult, e.g.; confident speaker or inability to communicate.

TOP PHALANGES – **INTELLECTUAL WORLD**

Vertical lines show mental skills – "The spark of inspiration". Externally, in relation to society; internally, in relation to self.

Horizontal lines show mental inhibitions and doubts - lack of vision. Externally, blocks to self-expression; internally, self-consciousness and lack of faith.

THE FINGERS – PSYCHOLOGICAL CHARACTERISTICS

THE THUMB
- **Long thumbs** show willpower, strength and reasoning ability.
- **Short thumbs** show lack of direction, poor judgement, insecurity.
- **Thick phalanges** indicate determination, stamina and domination.
- **Thin phalanges** indicate subtlety, diplomacy, strategy, economic use of willpower.

Top Phalange
Well-developed – good willpower, determination and sense of purpose.
Deficient – lack of willpower, laziness and weakness.
Stunted- indications frustration, sudden anger and difficulties in communication.

Middle Phalange
Long – thoughtfulness, reasoning abilities.
Short – acting instinctively.
Thick-set – honesty, bluntness, lack of diplomacy.
Waisted – diplomatic, compassionate, caring, discriminating – "the good listener".

Base Phalange
Over-developed – voluptuousness, lust, unbridled passions.
Well-developed – Joie de vivre, passionate, refined.
Under-developed – cool, calm, dispassionate.

THE INDEX FINGER – **Jupiter**
- **Long** index fingers show ego, leadership skills, confidence and determination
- **Short** index fingers show insecurity, lack of confidence – "The Victim".

Top Phalange
Well-developed - charisma, idealism, vision and faith.
Deficient – dogma, fanaticism, bigotry and inferiority.

Middle Phalange
Well-developed – business acumen, management skills, organisation.
Deficient – spendthrift, unfocused behaviour, inability to be methodical.

Base Phalange
Well-developed – love of food, drinks, power, earning money.
Deficient – deprivation, starvation, homelessness, poverty.

THE SECOND FINGER – **Saturn**
- **Long** second fingers show responsibility, honour, duty and justice.
- **Short** second fingers show social deprivation, anarchy and criminal behaviour.

Top Phalange:
Well-developed – The Philosopher, judge, novelist, researcher.
Deficient – lack of social position, political dissidence.

Middle Phalange:
Well-developed – administrative skills, property management, career vocation.
Deficient – disorganized, unconventional, inability to accept responsibility.

Base Phalange:
Well developed – craftsmanship, practical skills, collecting.
Deficient – inability to make things, loss of home, money, property.

THE THIRD FINGER – Sun [**Apollo**]
- **Long** third fingers show perfectionism, artistic or communication skills.
- **Short** third fingers show gambling, lust, social irresponsibility.

Top Phalange:
Well-developed – vision, linguistics, teaching, public vocations.
Deficient – lack of social skills and creative expression.

Middle Phalange:
Well-developed – accuracy, precision, discrimination, economy.
Deficient – untidiness, unruly– "The Dreamer".

Base Phalange:
Well-developed – fashion, life-style, artistic capabilities.
Deficient – anti-social behaviour, carelessness, loss of social identity.

THE FOURTH FINGER – **Mercury**
- **Long** fourth fingers show spiritual, scientific or social communication.
- **Short** fourth fingers show infantilism, childishness, shyness.

Top Phalange:
Well-developed – oration, speech, abstract thought.
Deficient – narrow-mindedness, lack of intuition.

Middle Phalange:
Well-developed – skills with either words or figures, e.g.; accountancy, singing, computers.
Deficient – inability to express oneself verbally.

Base Phalange:
Well-developed – financial skills, good communication skills.
Deficient – insecurity, lack of money, work prospects.

PHILOSOPHY OF CHIROLOGY

Inevitably such as ancient form of chirology have philosophical elements in it. The human hand is a container of consciousness, a means of self-expression (namely through the fingers). To a fortune teller, palmistry predicts; to certain doctors the hand may be used to diagnose neural dysfunctions or physical illnesses; to the practitioner of acupuncture the hand may be used to heal medical problems. Many eminent men, including Julius Caesar, Napoleon and Nostradamus have sought knowledge from the hand.

Why should palmistry counselling not be accredited with praise and acclaim? Using deductive logic and research certain criteria have been proved by exhaustive analysis to apply to the human hand. In China their form of chirology has been connected with acupuncture, herbal medicine which produced naturopathy, osteopathy and physiotherapy.

Chirology has as its aim the unification of body, mind and soul, or enlightenment. To gain this goal we should seek to become whole and express the oneness which is apparent in a balanced individual.

In ancient times geomancy or spiritual engineering was applied to the land. Ley lines conducted Ki or psychic energy throughout the Earth. They harmonised the geography of the land. Today such things are forgotten or made the subject of superstitions, e.g.; Stone Henge, the Glastonbury Tor, the Pyramid of Cheops. However in similar ways the lines carry our spiritual or Chi energy across the territory of the hand.

BODY AND MIND LANGUAGE

Body and mind are indivisibly linked. That which is present in the consciousness of the subject is reflected in their hand; more obviously in the movement of hands in communication – gesture. The hand expresses to the external world our thought, emotions and aspirations.

Metaphysically, what we read in the hand are the experiences of a person's life. Specifically time has a great effect upon this process. Our minds record details; our emotions' impressions. We live in the present but our minds record the past and our body posture reflects what we have learnt. Our past (what we have been) impinges upon our present (what we are) and is projected into the future, through what we hope or expect to become.

In the hand we may notice a person's inhibitions which are the result of negative past events. These may include shocks, such as the death of our parents or other factors that have acted upon the growth of our personalities. We may overcome these setbacks, indicated by dots, crosses or stars on the palm, by achieving a greater awareness of ourselves and responding to present difficulties with a greater perspective of the past. In addition, through psychotherapy, yoga or physical fitness we may learn to correct our body posture and better integrate our characters. A perceptive palmistry counsellor realises these imbalances and seeks to positively show the person their potential and means of stabilising their lives.

Palmistry counselling teaches us to notice the past, observe the present and gauge the future events. However during our lives the shape of our hands and the lines on it change and alter. Philosophically this is because people have free will. They do not only adapt to changing circumstances but often participate and sometimes instigate those changes. In particular by applying hand analysis we can observe in a person's hand their psychological attitude to inward and outward experiences.

A mistake made by many psychic palmists who have not studied chirology is to predict trends e.g.; a journey across water or descriptions of offspring. These are often inaccurate because they are based purely upon psychic abilities alone and are not verifiable in the hand.

That is not to say that a person's soul is unaware of destiny but their present day consciousness may not be able to channel to this potential. A wise palmistry counsellor interprets and analyses trends, firstly examining past events. In this way, present and future follow certain clearly defined patterns, proceeding from one another. Also outward events are mirrored by inner events forming a compass indicating the directions in one's life. Our thoughts, emotions and body language all colour the geographical map of the palm. Remember always that palmistry counselling is a holistic therapy, not a predictive tool, because the skills developed, move beyond the paradigm of solely divination

GESTURES

When analysing gestures the most important thing is to observe. The way a person uses their hands in self-expression is fundamental and impulsive and the language of gesture, as with facial expression, is universal.

The hands may be used in many ways; one of the most apparent gestures is when one shakes hands. Normal hands squeeze gently indicates a warm response. Some people grip the hand attempting to crush the fingers. This is not the sign of a truly healthy, strong person [who is often gentle], but indicates a compulsive individual, possibly attempting to compensate for feelings of inferiority. When a person gives a warm handshake, with a sparkling look in their eyes, this is an indication of sex appeal. Large flabby hands that perspire indicate a person who feels insecure, not physically strong, and may "live on their nerves".

Next, notice how a person holds their hands naturally. Slightly curled hands that swing naturally when walking seem most alive. Hands may be held lifelessly by the sides. Other hands may be closed in a fist. Unless the thumb is enclosed within the fingers this is the sign for a dynamic person with drive and personality. Upon death, the thumb often curls onto the palm to indicate that their will has surrendered to the Divine Will of God, and their consciousness ascended to the spiritual realms.

Finally look at the acts of self-expression. Jerky movements indicate nervousness and lack of co-ordination. Notice how some people point the index finger; this is a sign of an ambitious person indicating a certain point. Clenched hands that pound a table indicate strength and a sense of purpose. Fingers that drum a table show irritation, impatience and boredom. Hands that wash one another show anxiety and inner turmoil. People who suck their thumbs when alone seem to wish to return to childhood and safety. Nail biting may show insufficient interest in dietary matters.

Some further points from an elemental standpoint:

Square Earth Hands are used sparingly and with economy often with clenched hands. They will use them to indicate fundamental, practical things. The "clenched fist" often expresses such feelings.

Conic Water Hands are often limp from the wrists and make fluent, flowing gestures, which explain how they are feeling.

Mental Air Hands often use fingers more. They make circular movements or allow the hands to form circles. They are expressing points of view, ideas or concepts of intellectual thought.

Spatulate Fire Hands may point the fingers or make quick movements of the hands. They may point the first finger when motivated or hold the finger or thumb together when gesticulating. Their hands are active and seek to influence others.

HAND TYPE CLASSIFICATION

There are two methods of defining hand types, according to eastern and western viewpoints but they both correspond.

SQUARE OR PRACTICAL HANDS -Earth

A person with this hand type is usually well balanced, pragmatic, reliable and conventional – simplicity of lifestyle is preferred. Such people like the countryside and are often talented in craftsmanship, or in a lady they make good housekeepers and may have a love of cookery. They can be exceptional "good neighbours"- able to fix the fence, do the gardening and still have time and energy to mend your roof; they do not mind serving their fellows. However they are cautious and reserved and often choose their partners not according to beauty but for practical companionship. They may like horticulture and be skilled in building, mining ore engineering.

In a lady, they may be excellent at typing, millinery and tailoring. They often have a "creative curve" on their palms, e.g.; a rounded hand. This gives them reserves of energy and imagination. They will need strength as other people often depend on them or exploit their willingness to serve.

CONIC OR EMOTIONAL HANDS - Water

Emotional type hands are sensitive, artistic and often show a sympathetic nature. They may love music or be drawn to a career requiring a vocational understanding of others' plights, such as to be found in nursing, religious orders or in helping animals. They have deep emotions, good memories and may excel in selling fashionable goods. They like travelling, learning a language and often study the occult – they may have psychic powers. They are often slim and fastidious or fat and jovial and prefer long hair. Physically they may be excellent athletes and nearly all enjoy swimming. The women are often beautiful with bright eyes, make excellent and versatile wives and may enjoy a large family, being especially fertile. They may be gullible or naïve, but are generous and understanding of others' faults. They may grow old with many grand-children and fine memories of adventures, as they love to tell tales – and not always true ones.

INTELLECTUAL OR PHILOSOPHICAL HANDS -Air

Intellectual people are thoughtful, versatile, and humorous and love inventing new gadgetry. They are usually diplomatic, sophisticated and intelligent. They are concerned with ideas rather than activity and often make great scholars in law, science or medicine. They enjoy discussing art and may become professional musicians or actors. However they can be fickle and changeable and are naturally unconventional.

They may make good philosophers, for they love debate and should be encouraged to take a responsible social role, perhaps that of a teacher. They are avid campaigners and often enter the field of politics or religion, wherein they will fight tirelessly for freedom of choice, human rights or that which they believe will contain the truth.

They often prefer a long courtship, wherein they can delve into their partner's mind. They also love to travel, excel in learning languages and may take up hobbies in photography or computing. The intellectual hand on a lady reflects a charming, graceful one who is a good talker – but she may also be fussy and fastidious and has a critical approach to life. They are usually perfectionists with strong moral values but have critical views. Such attributes may be found with the intellectual hand.

SPATULATE OR ENERGETIC HANDS -Fire

Activity is of fundamental importance to people with speculate hands. Fire may warm – or flame and scorch; likewise these people can love. They are generous and optimistic or aggressive, troublesome and argumentative.

They can be creative or destructive, according to which mood they are in. They loathe routine work and feeling frustrated and limited. They are happiest when on their own. They like challenges, fuelling political debates and often inspire others. Their lives are a roller-coaster of delight or fear.

They may like the services, e.g.; army, navy, air force, or prefer to work in industry, engineering or work involving tools. The ladies may become competent secretaries, excellent hostesses or travel couriers, as they love warm countries.

In affection they are loving and generous, but may quarrel overmuch. They are rebellious and often require a cause to work for. In old age they sometimes put on weight (because they love rich food) and have circulatory problems. They make the best of friends and the worst of enemies. They must learn to rest and take up sports to channel their energies constructively.

PROFESSIONAL PALMIST'S REFERENCE TABLE

CELESTIAL ELEMENTAL ATTRIBUTES	EARTH Materialism; physical Structure	WATER Emotional responses; intuition; spirituality	AIR Intellectual; mental abilities	FIRE Energetic; dynamic capabilities	ETHER Divine will; soul world manifestation
PLANETARY SYMBOLISM	SATURN Taurus; Virgo; Capricorn Fixed; Mutable; Cardinal	THE MOON; NEPTUNE; VENUS; PLUTO Pisces; Cancer; Scorpio Mutable; Cardinal; Fixed	MERCURY; URANUS Gemini; Aquarius; Libra Mutable; Fixed; Cardinal	THE SUN; MARS Leo; Sagittarius; Aries Fixed; Mutable; Cardinal	STELLAR CONSTELLATIONS
HAND TYPES (Structure)	Square/Practical	Conic/Artistic	Intellectual/ Philosophical	Energetic/ Spatulate	PSYCHIC
FINGER TIPS (Mental Skills)	Pragmatic; methodical	Intuitive; instinctive	Reasoning; debating	Dynamic; inspirational	DIVINE MIND
FINGER PRINTS (Psychological Orientation)	Acts or service (physical or social)	Acts of adaptation (communing)	Acts of Individualism (fixity of ideals)	Acts of actuation (movement, growth)	DIVINE MIND
SKIN TYPES	I serve society	I relate to society	I educate society	I create change in society	BELIEF IN GOD
MOUNTS	I inspire to build	I inspire spirituality	I inspire communication	I inspire evolution	THE THUMB
FINGERS	Finger of Saturn	Finger of Jupiter	Finger of Mercury	Finger of Apollo	THE THUMB
MAJOR LINES	LIFE LINE Physical body (strength) (skeletal/muscular system)	HEART LINE Emotional life (fluidity) (glandular/lymphatic System)	HEAD LINE Mental life (brain, nervous system)	APOLLO LINE Energy for life (heart, circulatory system)	CREATION
MINOR LINES	Ring of Saturn	Ring of Solomon Line of Intuition Girdle of Venus	Medical Stigmata Teacher's Square	Line of Ambition Partnership lines	CREATION

SPECIAL NOTE: Hand-shape type does not necessarily relate to Zodiac Sign, but to attributes of the signs.

John Harrison 1995 –Copyright Note! This chart may not be reproduced in any form without prior permission from the Author.

CHIROGNOMY – STRUCTURE OF THE HAND

The structure of the hand is made up of bones called metacarpal bones. Also of three different types of nerve systems; radical, radial and ulna proximal.

The palm of the hand represents our physical nature, endurance, strength, our childhood, character and personality and our experiences of life. The fingers represent our ideas, feelings and indicate the way in which our energies are channelled. The height and width of the mounts indicate the quantity and quality of our creative energy.

The hand can be divided into four sections (see diagram). These indicate:

A – Our passive consciousness.

B – Our active consciousness.

C – Our passive awareness (sub-conscious).

D – Our active awareness.

By sub-conscious we mean latent abilities, e.g.; an instinctive understanding of musical notes.

The thumb represents our instincts and direction in life, religiously our "Guardian Angel". Too many lines show too much activity. Equally, large hands indicate the capacity to work in detail, e.g.; as in dentists, surgeons or research scientists. Small hands indicate the opposite. These people have large plans and are usually well organised, e.g.; businessmen, film directors, generals.

Short fingers are often found on extroverts, who organise large plans. Long fingers are found on introverts or specialists who use great detail.

Line patterns are a symbol of a person's communication with the macrocosm, or Universe; their activity within it and relationship to it. Fingerprint patterns, skin ridge patterns and skin texture indicate the microcosm, e.g.; how we function psychologically, socially and in our relationships. We act as we think and feel and the structure of the hand contains what we are capable of – our potential.

AN INTRODUCTION TO THE ELEMENTS

Palmistry is but one section of an ancient philosophy – that of alchemy. This consisted of the transmutation of metals into gold. Transposed onto a spiritual level, this sought to discover the philosopher's stone. In modern society metaphysical heurism, physiology and eugenics comprise the major field of study.

The position of the arteries in the body and the nerve endings in the hand provide the basis for examining the sensory passages from brain to hand. These link the conscious and unconscious elements of our beings and together with the circulatory vessels of the body provide insight into how the hand becomes a container and conductor of universal life force energy. In oriental chirology certain pressure points are used in acupressure and acupuncture to investigate health ailments.

Since early times the hand has been the tool of mankind. Nature and the seasons seem to affect our temperaments and with the similarity between science and religion in light of the advances in particle physics and the chaos theory which confirm the truth of ancient mystical teachings regarding the nature of the Universe, greater analysis has been possible. As we have evolved we have adapted to the forces of change, become more aware through our human potential as conscious beings and have begun to found our lives according to tour discoveries; we have developed, changed and become more evolved. Finally we found our spiritual awareness at higher level.

Therefore, this process of changeless change, produces the following metaphysical analogy:-

FOUNDATION – ADAPTATION – AWARENESS – EVOLUTION

ELEMENTAL DIVISIONS

For the purpose of analysis the hand is divided up into four segments according to the properties: practical, intellectual, energetic and emotionally responsive, representing qualities in human life. The following is a brief table of elemental attributes.

FIGURE TWO: QUADRANT DIVISIONS

A -   Passive Consciousness - *Feminine*
B -   Passive Awareness (Sub-Conscious) - *Feminine*
C -   Active Awareness - *Masculine*
D -   Passive Consciousness - *Masculine*

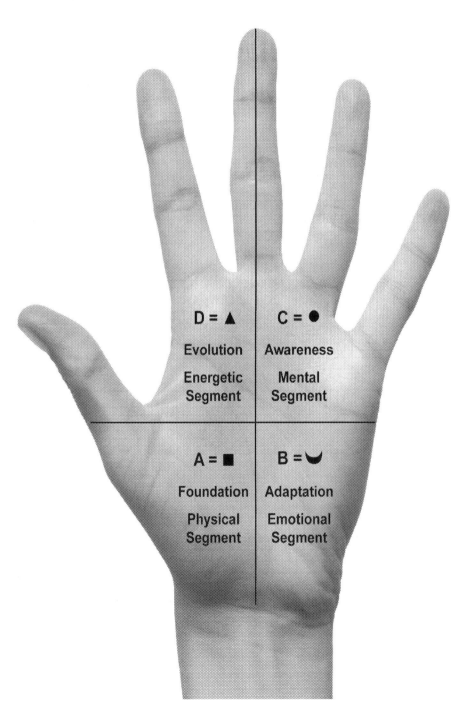

SEGMENT ANALYSIS

The hand may be divided into various compartments. The hand may be divided into four spheres. These represent the following:

  A.   THE SQUARE – FOUNDATION – THE PHYSICAL SEGMENT
  B.   THE CRESCENT – ADAPTATION – THE EMOTIONAL SEGMENT
  C.   THE CIRCLE – AWARENESS – THE MENTAL SEGMENT
  D.   THE TRIANGLE – EVOLUTION – THE ENERGETIC SEGMENT
  E.

THE PHYSICAL SEGMENT – FEMININE

Representing our homes, families, loyalty and sense of responsibility to society, our nation, this world called Earth. Also our biological rhythms, our strength and bone structure. Herein we also must consider our identities, our sense of harmony and the purely physical nature and bodily functions.

THE EMOTIONAL SEGMENT – FEMININE

Representing our subconscious dreams, our intuition and imagination, together with any love of art, music or creative expression. Also that which is mysterious and secretive - the unknown. Biologically, our blood and lymphatic systems – the fluidity of the body. Herein we delve into our psychic natures.

THE MENTAL SEGMENT – MASCULINE

Representing our thoughts, the results of which we use to comprehend material reality. Furthermore that which our images create and aspire towards. Organisation and reasoned planning. Biologically our lungs and respiratory system and ability to communicate, either verbally (linguists) or technologically ie telecommunications, as well as our sympathetic and parasympathetic nervous system. These are air attributes, as expressions of our minds and our intelligence.

THE ENERGETIC SEGMENT – MASCULINE

Representing our self-consciousness, ego and separate identities. All that inspires us, our ideals, our sense of freedom. Our philosophical passions, our scientific endeavours, our religious strivings and our hunting instincts. Most importantly our desire to know, feel and experience new things. Biologically our heart and circulatory systems (the creator and distributor of energy)

MAJOR LINE VARIATIONS

LINE OF VITALITY – LIFE LINE – EARTH

A   Wide Separation (1cm +) of **life and head lines** – strong independent person, possibly selfish.

B   **Very wide set life line** (moves into emotional segment) – overindulgence in food, drink and/or sex

C   **Wide set life line** – extrovert tendencies, e.g.; passionate enjoyment of life (creativity, music, arts, food, drink, entertainment)

D   **Narrow set life line** – introverted tendencies e.g.; careful, prudent [diet or money], discriminating, dispassionate, cautious, potentially reclusive

E   **Broken life line, sending branch back to fate line** – major change in lifestyle e.g.; career, relationships or health (note inner line of Mars).

F   **Forked life line, branching on to Luna mount** – restlessness, desires, for change, possible emigration or living in a foreign country.

LINE OF MENTALITY – HEAD LINE – MERCURY- AIR

A   **Long, high set head line** – rational, logical reasoning skills; perceptive problem solving abilities. Psychological understanding.

B   **Long, low set head line** – imaginative, inventive, excellent vision. Designing skills. Emotional empathy. Intuitive actions.

C   **Very short high set head line** – simple minded, mundane, impatient, impetuous (sudden anger?). Instinctive actions.

D   **Simian lines (head and heart line joined)** – positive: perseverance, concentration, focusing, single mindedness, public service. Negative: intensity, obsessions, compulsions, calculation, criminal tendencies in extreme cases, as with short stunted thumb tips.

E   **Short, low set head line** – instinctive, emotional responses, imagination acted upon, sensitive, sympathetic, compassionate, harmonious in love. Impetuous, moody, impatient

F   **Extremely low set, long head line** – spiritual gifts, strong intuition, empathy, impressionistic, extreme sensitivity. Occasionally manic depression or in extreme cases, lunacy or suicide.

LINE OF EMOTIONS – HEART LINE – VENUS -WATER

A   **Long, high set heart line ending in mount of Jupiter** – the philanthropic, humanitarian, charitable, compassionate. Strong, idealistic, beliefs tied to emotional, loving care.

B   **Short, low set heart line** – cool, dispassionate, undemonstrative, mental approach to loving. Occasionally selfish and thoughtless.

C   **High set heart line ending between index and second fingers** – demonstrative in affection, sympathetic, passionate. Usually unselfish, emotionally responsive.

D   **Long, low set heart line (with unbroken Girdle of Venus)** – detachment, undemonstrative; deep, repressed emotions. Strong, dreams, fantasies. Physical undemonstrative lust. Capable of role playing. Intense, underlying emotions. Secretiveness.

E   **Islanded heart line or dots on heart line** – either emotional confusion, disillusionment, traumas in love or health problems with heart or lungs, e.g.; asthma, or if dots present, heart attacks. Look at these features in conjunction with the life line – chronology.

LINE OF STABILITY – FATE LINE- SATURN

A   **Long, unbroken, commencing on mount of Luna** – successful career, possibly in creative field, or in service to the public. Dependent upon goodwill.

B   **Multiple broken line** – either an insecure person, lacking stability, always changing jobs, moving house or changing relationships or health problems where the physical or psychological health is impaired and instability in life prevails.

C   **Strong line above head line** – career success after 40 years of age.

D   **Strong, unbroken, commencing on mount of Neptune** – vocational line – success attained through perseverance, strength, dedication, discipline. Often these people are the "backbone" supporters of their family or work colleagues.

E   **Long unbroken line inside of life line**- supporting or supported by the family to attain success.

LINE OF CREATIVITY – APOLLO LINE- SUN

A   **Long, unbroken line, commencing on mount of Neptune** – a successful life of public service and devotion. Responsible government of resources.

B   **Long, unbroken line, commencing on mount of Luna** – a successful life with creative brilliancy; dependent upon public acclaim (often found on the hands of actors, entertainers, prominent politicians, etc).

THE HEALTH OF THE HAND

Illness is represented in the hand by imbalance and may be physical or psychological. Basically these imbalances can be observed in the shape of the hand, the nails, and the mounts, the fingers or the lines of the hand; and disease can be diagnosed from skin ridge patterns.

This area of study speaks volumes alone and so will be treated briefly so as not to confuse the reader with ramifications and terminology exclusive to the medical profession.

Firstly, we should note the shape of the knuckles. When pronounced with the index knuckle prominent it indicates a violent nature (excellent in the hand of a boxer).

Then observe the colour of the hand. A general guide is as follows:
Normal hands are pink (except when temperature varies, according to climate or metabolism).

Here we adhere to the Four Types of Humors, related in Alchemy, to the Elements .
MELANCHOLIC   CHOLERIC   PHLEGMATIC   SANGUINE.
Melancholic is represented by black bile; Choleric by yellow bile; Phlegmatic by phlegm;
Sanguine by blood. These mirror the emotions that relate to the health of individuals. "

Red hands - Sanguine - AIR typical illnesses in these people.

Yellow hands - Phlegmatic - WATER typical illnesses in these people.

White hands - Choleric -FIRE - typical illnesses in these people.

Blue hands - Melancholic - EARTH - typical illnesses in these people.

Red hands (energetic type) - typical illnesses in these people

These show intensity and a person inclined towards excesses of addictions i.e.; alcohol or drugs. Fever, swellings, cuts and inflammations may be observed. The blood may be thin; lung ailments are possible of which bronchitis and pneumonia are examples.

Yellow hands (practical type) – typical illnesses in these people

A person with such hands may be irritable, nervous and temperamental. Biliousness and constipation may be present. The liver and gallbladder and its malfunctions are the cause. In addition, a person may suffer from spinal problems, brittle bones and eye ailments.

White hands (intellectual type) – typical illnesses in these people

They illustrate a lack of vital energy, causing fatigue, listlessness and possible paralysis. The hearing may also be inefficient. People who die of exposure or drowning also have white hands.

Blue hands (emotional type) – typical illnesses in these people

These indicate a lack of fluidity in the body. Skin ailments, poor circulation and dysfunctions of the lymphatic glands may be apparent. Smoking and excessive drinking cause blue hands.

MISCELLANEOUS EXAMPLES OF ILL-HEALTH

NAILS

These should be smooth and pliable. Fluting indicates nervous disorders and is often found on the hands of heavy smokers.

White spots indicate mineral deficiencies.

Short, round fingernails show heart ailments; when moons are lacking and the nails are bluish then a heart attack may be imminent.

Shell shaped nails show an allergic nature; it also forebodes long illnesses and fainting, blackouts or paralysis. **Large oval** nails show lung complaints, and problems with the digestive system.

Long thin nails show spinal problems. **Deep dark** nails show blood pressure problems.

The palmar region may also be an indication of health problems. An illness may be wedded to a person's chronology (to give exact time of illness).

Especially note the Mercury line (for organic deterioration), the line of emotions (for heart defects or emotional imbalances), the line of mentality (for mental disorders) and the ring of Venus.

Stars, crosses, dots and grille formations together with islands combine to cause ill-health.

The Via Lascivious may also indicate a reaction to toxic substance, food allergies or addictions.

FIGURE THREE: HEALTH IN THE HAND

A - Throat
B - Ears
C - Spine
D - Lungs
E - Heart
F - Eyes
G - Internal Liver
H - Child Birth (Complications)

1 Change of lifestyle
2 Metabolic sensitivity
3 Death at 70
4 Divorce
5 Heart Attack (dots)
6 Head Injury (Motorcycle accident)

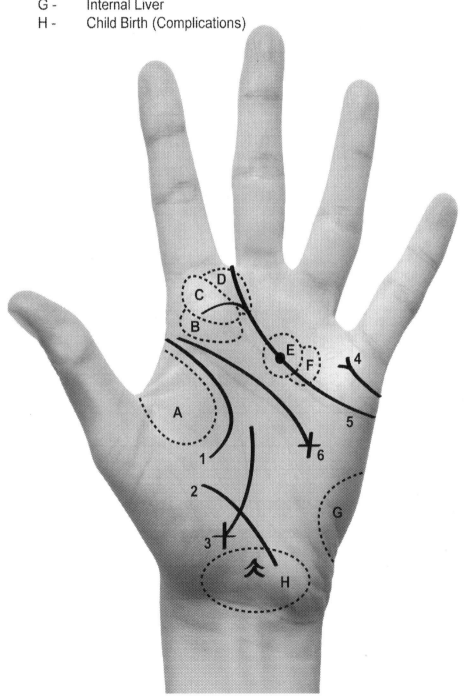

HOW TO TAKE HAND PRINTS

MATERIALS REQUIRED: _
1. A tube of Rodney's water soluble block printing colour or lipstick (dark red, black or purple.]
2. A small roller (as used for lithographic printing, obtainable from art stores). Also a large wall tile or piece of linoleum.
3. Hairspray (to use as a fixative).
4. 4 sheets of white computer paper (10 gsm or thicker), of A4 format
5. A dark felt tip pen or pencil.
6. Cotton Wool.

METHOD 1 – Do this on a table.
1. Place one sheet of paper on a table with a small quantity of cotton wool underneath in the centre (which will fit the natural hollow of your hand when placed upon it).
2. Squeeze a small toothpaste-sized quantity of colour on to the tile and roll it out. Using the roller, apply ink evenly to all parts of palm (or apply lipstick evenly to the palm and fingers).
3. Relax your hand and place it in a natural manner on the paper, gently pressing down on fingers and thumb. Then draw around your hand with the pencil and slowly lift your hand off the page (Check for clarity of prints).
4. Apply more ink (or lipstick) if required. Then place the tops of fingers/thumbs on the bottom of the pages and make prints, not forgetting to draw around these and mark them i.e.; Thumb; 1st; 2nd; 3rd; 4th fingers as appropriate.
5. Spray your two complete sets of prints (two of each hand) with hairspray, or fixative

METHOD 2
1. Go to a store that has a photocopier. Photostat each hand separately by placing hand on the glass and closing over it. Use low to medium setting. (CHECK FOR CLARITY OF PRINTS!)

1. **Now Prepare your handprints as shown**
2. **METHOD ONE –How to produce hand digital photos.**

3. This is by far the quickest, easiest and less messy of the methods. You will ideally need someone to take the photos for you

4. 1. Place your hands in front of a dark background i.e. not light coloured.

5. Take 2 photos, one of each hand and one set of each finger-print pattern (including thumbs) angled straight on i.e. not side views.

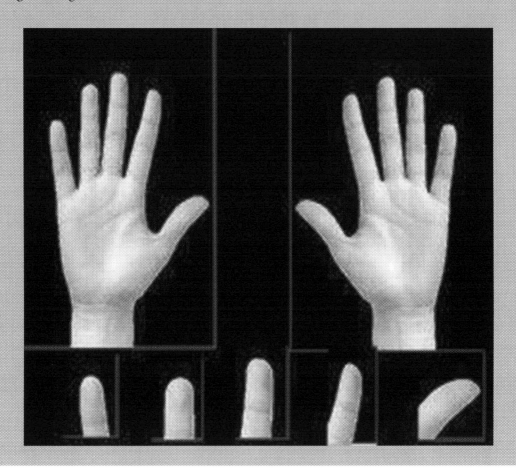

YOUR FIRST PROFESSIONAL READING

There are three methods of reading the hands:-
A – Analysis of handprints, via Mail.
B – A personal client consultation
C - Digital Photography Reading via e mail.

ANALYSIS OF THE HAND

In order to analyse a person's handprints, three things are essential;
A – An excellent handprint which is detailed and has clarity of shape, line formations and skin ridge patterns.
B – The ability to perceive, observe and deduce facts for the spatial dimensions of the hand, the lines, mounts and fingerprint patterns.
C – The capacity to distil the essential ingredients presented by the chirognomical features and chiromantic regions and summarise these succinctly and diplomatically to your client, via e mail, recording device or in writing, in the form of counselling – always remembering the cardinal rule – "How can I help this person to improve their life?"

HAND READINGS IN PERSON

Proceed with your analysis of the hand shape noting finger spacing and settings.
This is followed by an in-depth assessment of the fingers and thumbs commencing with the thumb.
Next feel the inner palms to determine skin textures.
Then examine the mounts and note any palmar skin ridge patterns.
In your detailed study of the lines; begin with the life line – check longevity, quality (thick or narrow), the colour, tone and depth. Note any breaks or miscellaneous line features, e.g.; crosses, squares, etc.
Do the same for the head line, heart line, fate line and line of creativity (sun line).
You will now have been looking at both hands in conjunction, bearing in mind that on right handed people i.e.; the majority of the population, the left hand represents development from childhood to adulthood and the right hand represents changes caused to or by your client, i.e.; what they do with their lives, for better or for worse.

In your summary you will be diplomatic and place yourself in your client's shoes, understand how you would feel in their circumstances. Personally, I never tell a client the truth where to do so would cause injury or turmoil.

You have great influence and must use it wisely with humour and compassion.

Conclude by thanking your client for the privilege of reading their hands and only when they are completely satisfied and you have answered all relevant questions, will you receive feedback, payment, or thanks.

THE ASSOCIATION OF PALMISTRY COUNSELLORS CODE OF CONDUCT

Becoming a palmistry counsellor is a serious undertaking. Palmistry counselling is a new profession utilising practical discipline, spiritual gifts and counselling skills and I actively encourage people from all walks of like to join my Association.

My students must not discriminate against clients on the ground of race, age, sexual orientation, religion or politics. In all aspects of their conduct, responsibility and ethical professionalism is essential.

Being a modern palmistry counsellor, I question those authorities whose skills that rely solely upon hand analysis or psychic impressions and inspire independent research in both study and into today's society.

Such limitations, represented by undeveloped skills, do not best serve the general public, nor provide the essential counselling support required for a professional therapy.

It is because I have studied metaphysics and esoteric philosophy, rather than solely science, that the profession that I have created, is founded upon the secure foundation of the wisdom of the ages.

Professional chirologists rely purely upon science, logic and hand analysis, and interpret but do not predict.

Psychics rely solely upon intuition, often without knowledge of chirology or counselling.

By contrast, palmistry counsellors base their professional skills, not only, upon chirology but the principles of metaphysics, as laid down by Cornelius Agrippa, Sir Isaac Newton, Paracelsus and Robert Fludd.

Personally, I am not a man of science, but of philosophy and spirituality. Over the centuries alchemy and magic have been replaced by atheism, agnosticism and paternalism, which in my view has resulted in the persecution of women, ethic minorities, spiritual aspirants, and independent thinkers.

The general public still seek out the "mystery of the hands"[palmistry], which divines the truth, accepting that we are spirits, living in the material world, and as such each of us, has a destiny to fulfil.

I encourage all my students to create their own independent research.

For those who are drawn to the spiritual path to enlightenment, I encourage you to find a Perfect Master [Sat Guru], who has proven credentials, and attain Liberation in this life. Should you wish to learn more about such a Path to Enlightenment, or to communicate with Enlightened Teachers [Adepts]; then you are welcome to contact me, and I would endeavour to answer any pertinent questions?

GLOSSARY OF TERMS

Chirology	-	the analytical study of hands
Chirognomy	-	the study of the shape of the hands
Hermetic	-	appertaining to the ancient philosophy of creation
Karma	-	the Laws of Cause and Effect
Macrocosm	-	Mankind observed as a component manifestation of divine consciousness
Microcosm	-	the manifestation in human consciousness of external cosmic phenomena
Ontology	-	the study of the essence of being
Palmistry	-	the art of hand divination – fortune telling

OTHER MISCELLANEOUS LINES
- Islands indicate disillusionment
- Bars and dots indicate barriers and shocks
- Tassels indicate dissipation of energy
- Wavy lines show vacillation
- Horizontal line show inhibitions
- Curved lines within the life line are influence lines, being parents or loved ones reinforcing a person's energy

MISCELLANEOUS PALMAR FEATURES

Islands   - periods of confusion or disillusionment.

Dots   - shocks/traumas either physical or psychological.

Wavy Lines   - vacillation, indecision, procrastination, hesitancy.

Crosses		- setbacks.
Stars		- violence, great trauma, e.g.; nervous breakdowns.
Squares		- protection, safety, preservation from harm.
Triangles		- good fortune, success.
Forks		- division of energies e.g.; divorce or separation
Breaks		- change of direction for good or ill.
Bars		- inhibitions, restraints, blocks.
Grilles		- struggle, lack of progress.

FEATURES ON FINGERS AND THEIR PHALANGES

Striations (vertical lines)	| | |	- talents, skills, abilities
Hyper-striations (many striations)	|||||	- stress, overwork
Bars	===	- inhibitions, blocks to achievement

MEANINGS OF FINGER PHALANGES

Base phalanges	- Practical, down-to-earth skills and abilities
Middle phalanges	-Executive, organisation, management skills
Top phalanges	- Mental or philosophical abilities

SUGGESTED RECOMMENDED BOOKS TO READ

= Good   **=Important   *=Excellent (the best!)

A.	Cheiro – Book of Fame and Fortune	**
B.	Annals of Human Genetics by Sir Francis Galton (EUGENICS)	**
C.	The Human Hand, the Living Symbol by Noel Jaquin	***
D.	Hands and Faces by Mrs Katherine Ashton	*
E.	The Science of Hand Reading Simplified by K.C. Sen	**
F.	The Hand in Psychological Diagnosis by C. Wolfe	***
G.	The Human Hand by Sir Charles Bell	***
H.	Laws of Scientific Hand Reading by W. Benham	***
I.	The Palmistry Work-Book by Nathaniel Altman	***
J.	The Theory of Metaphysical Influence by N. Jacquin	***
K.	The Hand reveals by Dylan Warren Davies	***
L.	How to Read Hands by Lori Reid	**
M.	Life Lines by Peter West	**
N.	Hand Psychology by Andrew Fitzherbert	***
O.	Practical Palmistry by David Brandon Jones	*
P.	The Encyclopaedia of Palmistry by M. Brockman	*
Q.	Discover Palmistry N. Altman	**
A.	Universal Hand Analysis by Magda Van Dijk Rijneke	***
R.	The Life in your Hands by Beryl Hutchinson	***
S.	The Book of Palmistry by Fred Getting's	**

Many excellent books are out of print. Seek out a good specialist second hand bookshop.

ADVANCED PALMISTRY COURSE TEST

Two clients, Sylvia Goldman and Paul Yeung, have decided to have a consultation.

Either provide a CD or mobile phone recording or type up your brief report paying special attention to how you would present your finding honestly but diplomatically to your clients in order to emphasise their positive strengths. I believe that all the information you require to successfully complete this test is contained within the Beginners and Advanced Courses. However, I have included my own brief perceptions underneath each "consultation".

CONSULTATION A – Sylvia Goldman

A neat Jewish lady, 45 years of age, 5' 2" tall with silver grey hair and piercing grey eyes. You notice she hold her hands clenched together when walking into your office. What does this tell you about her?

You notice that she has speculate hands with knotty second joints. What will be the shape of her palms?

Her skin texture is silky and smooth. What is her skin type?

Her fingers are close held with a high-set thumb. What do these characteristics mean?

Her index finger is short on her left hand but long on her right. How would you interpret this change?

Her life line is long. Her head line is separated from her life line, long and high-set. Decide on what this will mean.

On her fingertips she has all loop print patterns, except the middle finger which have whorls. Suggest what this means?

MY SUGGESTED ANSWERS
- A) Clenched hands – energetic, dynamic.
- B) Spatulate hands – active doer.
- C) Knotty fingers – enjoys arguing, debating, reasoning.

D) Silky skin emotional, responsive in social relationships.

E) Fingers close held – cautious.

F) High set thumb - aesthetic/intellectual interests.

G) Index fingers – she used to lack confidence in herself, now she is more assertive.

H) Fingerprints - sociable, adaptable, gregarious, however, she had a strong sense of justice, unusual working life (whorl patterns).

I) High set separated life and heart lines – independence, head rules the heart.

CONSULTATION B – Paul Yeung

Your second client Paul is a slim, elegant Chinese gentleman, 25 years of age with long dark hair and smiling eyes. He speaks quickly and gesticulates using his index finger.

What does this tell you about him?

He has long, narrow palms with long slim fingers.

What is his hand shape?

His index finger and little finger are both short. However the base phalanges on the index finger and middle finger are large.

What does this mean?

He has a long, low set head line and a long high set heart line extending onto the mount of Jupiter. His Girder of Venus is broken and a line descends from the base of the finger of Apollo across the heart line into the life line.

With these feature, how would you expect Paul to relate to other within society?

MY SUGGESTED ANSWERS

A) Gesticulating index finger – the desire for leadership.

B) Hand shape – conic – artistic/emotional hands.

C) Index and little fingers - lacking confidence; feelings of insecurity, a youthful approach to life.

D) Low set head line – creative, artistic – the emotions rule over mentality.

E) High set heart line – a humanitarian, compassionate person.

F) Broken Girdle of Venus plus extensor line – Paul is Gay.

G) Base phalanges well developed – he works as a chef and is also a craftsman.

BIOGRAPHY OF THE AUTHOR - JOHN HARRISON

Born in West London, John possessed the "intuitive gifts" since childhood of clairvoyance, clairsentience and visions. Being naturally creative he wrote poetry from an early age and later short stories and songs. Although not academically bright, due to dyslexia, he studied English, Religion, Law and Politics but chose to go into retail and sales management as his first career path.

However, John's main interest was always in religion and spirituality. In his teenage years he studied astrology and palmistry and began practicing yoga, meditation and Tai Chi Chuan, being fascinated by Taoism and Hinduism. This found fruition when he became the Chairman of the Theosophical Society (Olcott Lodge) organising and attending lectures by the leading religious authorities of those days. He also lectured himself having written his thesis on palmistry counselling, the profession he was to found.

Not content to just be just a student, having experienced his first "samadhi" in 1978; which is an expanded state of consciousness, John began a lifelong quest to discover the truth of being and the path to self- realisation and spiritual enlightenment. He learnt that in all the major religions there were references to the Word of God, (sound vibrations) and Knowledge of God - Gnosis (light frequencies). Whilst this philosophy is intellectually appealing, the truth is that the mind never becomes enlightened.

So began the quest to find a Perfect Master who could reveal by their Grace, the Truth of Being. Having participated in a whole succession of "spiritual paths" where teachers purported to take the aspirant on a journey to enlightenment but then failed to mention that they themselves were not enlightened, many illusions were experienced.

On the work front, regrettably subsequent to recession and austerity, our family retail business reached its nemesis in 1988 when my parents Alan and Joyce retired. Unemployed for the first time in years, I took this opportunity to travel around the world, experiencing many diverse cultures, revelling in their customs, traditions and spiritual ceremonies. Upon my return I began to train as an aromatherapist and spiritual healer, going on to become a psychotherapist, hypnotherapist, Seichem Tera Mai Healing Master as well as studying Tantra and Chi Kung. With this experience, I started the Smile Holistic Practice.

In 1989 whilst travelling in India I was involved in a major road traffic accident but miraculously escaped virtually unscathed. Upon returning to England, I sought treatment myself at a local mind, body and soul exhibition. It was a wonderful experience and I found out then that such exhibitions occurred all over the United Kingdom, where tarot readers, clairvoyants and palmists could earn a living by giving readings to an appreciative public.

Over successive years I have been published in leading magazines such as Kindred Spirit and Here's Health as well as appearing on national T.V. and radio. I have given lectures on palmistry counselling in the U.S.A. where my exemplary knowledge and experience dispelled many of the myths about palmistry and I was accorded great respect by their chirology teachers, who sent their students to purchase my home tuition palmistry counselling manuals and have readings.

Palmistry counselling is the new career that I have founded. It is a collaboration of the skills of hand analysis (chirology) married to the art of hand divination (palmistry) which is rooted in the philosophy of hermeticism, alchemy, metaphysical heurism and ontology. The psychological insights provided by possessing qualifications in this medium, or psychotherapy, then provide the framework for palmistry counselling. Palmistry counselling is a therapeutic discipline aimed at empowering clients to attain their full potential in the fields of health, careers and relationships.

In conclusion, palmistry counselling is a practical discipline offering insights into our purpose in life.

For those seeking answers to questions a good grounding in metaphysics and philosophy is necessary.

Then beyond palmistry counselling can be found the path to self- realisation and spiritual enlightenment.

Palmistry Counselling

For private readings, party bookings, exhibition or corporate events, articles, lectures, T.V or radio appearances or to learn palmistry counselling contact John Harrison at his website:
www.john-harrison-palmistry.com
Email:smile4u2024@yahoo.co.uk

Meditation and Spiritual Development

To learn to relax, release stress, and find peace, serenity, balance and equanimity or to go on the journey leading to self- realisation and spiritual enlightenment, visit my website:
www.meditation-4u2.com

CHI KUNG

To gain a good grounding in Taoist Philosophy, learn Standing and Moving Postures, how to store Chi, Inner Smile Meditation and Healing Sounds.

Seichem Tera Mai Healing Courses and Treatments

Learn to rejuvenate, re-energise, and heal yourself or others. One to one sessions, healing courses/ workshops available from this experienced Seichem Master.
www.smileholistictherapies.com
Email: - smile4u2024@yahoo.co.uk

SMILE HOLISTIC PRACTICE
MEDITATION CLASSES
(relax, feel peace, discover the real you!)

REIKI HEALING COURSE/TREATMENTS
(rejuvenate, re-energise, learn to heal yourself and others)

PALMISTRY COUNSELLING
(guidance on health, careers, relationships, private readings,
party bookings, tuition and lectures)

MEDITATION

A PATH TO ENLIGHTENMENT

TRUE MEDITATION

True meditation begins when thoughts cease.
This unique meditation occurs on a Path to Enlightenment
Where the answers to our fundamental questions are resolved.
This becomes a medium for the exploration of human nature and our identity.
In order to discover the Truth of our Being we need to meditate upon this Life Stream.
The source of life can be perceived in meditation as a beautiful radiance and audible vibrancy.
Heard without hearing, seen without looking, this energy stream is accompanied
by a Bliss, Tranquillity and a Serenity that is almost impossible to imagine!
Now there is no need to look outside ourselves for validation or reassurances
As we can come to know that this radiance is not only a part of our nature,
But the very essence of our Being.

If you are interested in meditation, simply go to our Web-site:

www.1meditation.com

"True Love is a form without a limit.
It is the real freedom all seek.
Bright like the Sun
Cool like the Moon
The Inner Light is revealed
To be our true path home"

MR JOHN HARRISON – MASTER PALMISTRY COUNSELLOR

E-mail: smile4u@yahoo2024.co.uk
Websites: http://john-harrison-palmistry.com
http://smileholistictherapies.com, http://meditation-4u2.com
*Postal Tuition Courses *Reading by email *Talks *Workshops*
*Events *Private Consultations *Party Bookings

With thanks to contributors
Images by http://www.scottgaunt.co.uk
Compiled by http://homebusinesszone.co.uk
Marketing & PR by http://karenperkinslifecoach.co.uk